Margaret Clitherow
Saint of York

by

John Rayne-Davis

Highgate of Beverley

Highgate Publications (Beverley) Limited
2002

All proceeds received by the author from this book are going to the St. Wilfrid's Church renovation fund

This book is dedicated to the memory of the many thousands of people murdered in the United States of America, in New York City and Washington DC, on 11 September 2001.

British Library Cataloguing in Publication Data.
A catalogue record for this book is available from the British Library.

© 2002 John Rayne-Davis

John Rayne-Davis asserts the moral right to be identified as the author of this work.

ISBN 1 902645 32 4

Published by

Highgate of Beverley

Highgate Publications (Beverley) Limited
4 Newbegin, Beverley, HU17 8EG. Telephone (01482) 886017

Printed by Highgate Print Limited
4 Newbegin, Beverley, HU17 8EG. Telephone (01482) 886017

Index

Foreword

In the Catholic Church of St. Wilfrid's, only a few hundred yards from York Minster, in the city centre, is a carved wooden statue of a young woman. She is in Tudor dress and is clearly a woman of some beauty. However, further inspection shows that this is no chocolate-box beauty, but a person of great force of character and personality. There is great kindness and compassion in the face, but also considerable strength.

This carved statue, which is of Italian origin, is perhaps one of the most attractive and sympathetic representations of a woman of great courage and deep religious conviction, Saint Margaret Clitherow, martyr of York. Margaret died in 1586 for her belief in the Catholic Church and also, as this book will show, to protect the lives of her family and friends.

Her sacrifice is as relevant today as when she lost her life over four hundred years ago. The times she lived in were known for their lack of tolerance of different religious beliefs and traditions. We may easily look back at this situation and marvel that people could murder one another simply because they followed the Catholic or Protestant path. We have only to recall the evil events of 11 September 2001 to see that religious prejudice is still alive and well.

Margaret was crushed to death, in a most horrific execution, quite simply because she refused to conform to the religious norms of her day. She stands as a shining example of great courage, integrity and, above all, an overpowering faith in God. Margaret Clitherow emerges as a most engaging and attractive personality, even after a period of four hundred years.

One of the greatest merits the saints afford us is that we can see reflections of ourselves and indeed our weaknesses in them. The type of saint who appears to be excessively pious and holy often tends to have very few devotees, quite simply because no one can live up to him or her! Often saints of this kind are left on their pedestals without much genuine love or admiration.

The greatest saints of the past have been essentially extremely human and even very vulnerable. One has only to remember Simon Peter to think of his impulsiveness: his temper coupled with the fact that he deserted his Master, when he was desperately needed. It is in this ordinary humanity that we can relate to the saints and through their weakness that they can lead us directly to God.

Margaret was a woman of deep compassion and understanding of others. She was a genuine friend in need, but she was also a born leader. However, she could be impulsive and had a temper. She had a zest for life and enjoyment that made her a very attractive and warm person to be with. Furthermore, she was a working housewife and therefore knew all the tensions and traumas of living in a family, as well as the joys this can bring. She was certainly a very honest and real person. She would have been amazed if anyone in her lifetime had described her as a saint. However, she also had a confidence and steel in her soul that singled her out as very special.

It was this that destined her for an extraordinary fate and vocation that, quite rightly, placed her among the company of God's saints. In Margaret Clitherow we see a woman who laid down her life, in her prime, for her God and to protect those closest to her. It is right that the Catholic Church is deeply proud of her supreme sacrifice, for without the martyrs of the sixteenth and seventeenth centuries it is debatable whether the Catholic Church would have survived in England.

It is unfortunately true that persecution has been the oxygen of Christian belief from the time of the Apostles. Indeed the Church has grown in numbers and spirituality much more in times when it was under threat and fighting for its very survival. It often tends to stagnate and lose its way when it becomes a comfortable bastion of the establishment.

It is important to remember that persecution has not been confined to Catholics. Many Protestants have died with great dignity and courage at the hands of Catholics for their firm belief in their tradition and in Almighty God. This book is not simply about the persecution of Catholics; it is about intolerance and prejudice from whatever direction it comes. Recent events have shown only too clearly this is an integral part of our world.

Margaret's legacy is greater than her contribution to Catholic belief and indeed survival. She represents the human spirit, inspired by the full force of God, standing out against the forces of evil, intolerance, prejudice and conformity. These elements are just as present today as they were in Tudor England. Indeed, they stretch back to the dawn of human history.

Margaret Clitherow is very relevant to the lives of all people living today and represents the human yearning for God.

"Jam hiems transiit, imber-
abiit, et recessit: surge, amica
mea, et veni." *—Off. Parv.*
B. Mariæ ad Vesperas.

St. Margaret Clitherow: frontispiece of William Nicholson (ed.), Life and Death of
Margaret Clitherow, The Martyr of York *(1849).*

The world that Margaret knew

It is virtually impossible for people living in the first years of the twenty-first century to understand and relate to the lifestyle and attitudes of sixteenth-century England.

It should be said straight away that this section of this book is not intended as a detailed social history of this period. The author is unqualified to undertake this. In any case there are many excellent books already covering it. Instead, it is intended to try and give the reader an idea of how ordinary people living through that time might have thought, and the sort of pressures (which were very different to ours) that affected their lives.

There is probably a rather hazy impression of life in the sixteenth century among people who have not studied the period in any depth. In part, very romanticised films and books compound this. In films actors wearing Tudor costumes often convey very modern, even 'politically correct' attitudes!

For example, there is a myth of 'Merrie England' with contented yokels dancing round a maypole. Furthermore, Henry VIII can be shown as a rather jovial, even loveable king, who basically had the good of his subjects at heart. Nothing could be further from the truth. In reality despotism existed which would make the most repressive South American dictator look positively benevolent. We live in an era in which it is fashionable to criticise, sometimes unfairly, those in authority. A particular target is the present Royal Family. It is worth considering that, if anyone in sixteenth-century England had expressed views that are currently fashionable, regarding any monarch of that time, they would have been instantly arrested for high treason and publicly executed within a few days.

Furthermore, the idea that the Elizabethan period was some kind of 'golden age' of enterprise, culture and exploration would have been laughed to scorn by people who lived at the time. The reality they saw was an under-populated country, with grinding poverty, and subject to virulent and deadly epidemics which could reduce the population by as much as 20%.

We might be excused for thinking the greatest barrier between ourselves and people living in the sixteenth century is our scope of technological development, such as computers, instant communication and travel across the world in a few hours. We might believe that people of that era would have stared in awe and wonder at our present lifestyle. It is much more likely that they would have dismissed modern technological progress as 'devilry, wizardry and the works of the evil one'. The difference between us and the people who lived at the time of Margaret Clitherow is not our scientific superiority; it is social and psychological.

Law and Order

Since Margaret was executed for holding religious views which did not conform to those acceptable to the State, it is interesting to look at the acceptance of justice and the laws of her time.

There must be very few people today who would agree with capital punishment for offences such as theft or forgery. However, both of these received the death penalty until the nineteenth century. Most people in Margaret's era would have dismissed our insistence on human rights as quite laughable.

Public executions of a most gruesome kind were common in England, and almost totally accepted. William Harrison described the situation in England in 1577. He states: 'In the reign of Henry VIII there were hanged seventy-two thousand thieves and rogues besides other malefactors.' This makes about two thousand people a year executed. However, the same author is quick to point out that in Elizabeth's time, there were only about four hundred a year hanged for theft or robbery.

The concept of Tudor despotism was no myth. Indeed, execution was strictly graded by social status in society. The headman's axe was reserved for those of nobility and high rank, while death by burning or hanging was the fate of countless people at the lower social levels.

Furthermore, public executions were an acceptable form of entertainment, probably on a par with a day out at the races in the twentieth century. Tudor England revelled in watching the death contortions of some poor unfortunate who had perhaps stolen a loaf of bread. This will explain why there was little outcry against the inhuman execution of Catholics (or Protestants under Mary). It was an acceptable part of life.

Public executions were extremely common in York, and the Knavesmire, where the gallows was situated, did steady business. The gallows in York was erected in 1379, and was called locally 'the three legged mare'. Among its most famous 'customers' was the highwayman, Dick Turpin. However, from 1537 onwards a new type of so-called criminal featured among its grisly list, namely those Catholics who opposed the supremacy of the monarch as head of the Church of England. Many priests and lay people of the Catholic faith ended their lives there over the next 150 years.

It was common practice to display the heads or dismembered limbs of so-called traitors on Micklegate Bar in York. Indeed, the road leading up to the Bar is called, to this day, Blossom Street. The origin of this name was that flowers and sweet-smelling shrubs were planted there in an attempt to remove the stench of rotting flesh.

Travel

We live in an era in which it is possible to travel across this country in a matter of a few hours, either on the excellent network of motorways or in the comfort of a train. At the time of Margaret Clitherow life travel was dramatically different.

The first road table of 1541 had only nine long-distance routes listed linking London with the main towns and cities of the kingdom. No cross-country routes existed. If a journey had been taken from York to Chester, this would have largely been on mere tracks between villages. These were little better than present-day farm tracks and could easily become a sea of mud during the winter months. Only the main roads in towns were cobbled. All other roads were dirt tracks kept firm by the passage of traffic. There was a statutory requirement for the upkeep of bridges by a parish. But this 'maintenance' was crude and basic when compared to its modern equivalent.

Only royalty or the nobility could afford to travel by coach and such vehicles were far from luxurious. Most coaches had no window protection, and their suspension was on a par with a farm cart. Among the merchant classes, such as Margaret's household, journeys would be taken on horseback. The poor had to travel on foot.

It was essential to be armed. Much of England was still forested and robbers brigands and 'masterless men' lurked in this natural cover to spring out and attack the unwary traveller. Murder and rape were commonplace, and rarely were these crimes punished, since those responsible could lose themselves in the woodlands. It was only about the time of Margaret's life that wolves were exterminated in England, so there were natural hazards as well as those of human agency. Overall, the countryside was not a place to linger in or enjoy.

Journeys were taken between isolated, wayside inns, most of which were of very doubtful character, and here again robbery was common. Before the Reformation monasteries provided the safest haven for the weary traveller but they had all been destroyed in Henry VIII's time.

Progress was pitifully slow and 12 to 15 miles quite a common distance to average in a day. To illustrate this a government official was sent post-haste from London to Berwick in 1539. He left the capital on 4 January, and took four days to reach Fotheringay in Northamptonshire. By 12 January he had reached Pontefract in Yorkshire. He finally arrived at Berwick on 28 January. Progress was obviously leisurely by comparison with today.

Religion

Religion forms the whole basis of Margaret Clitherow's life and death. Without the fervour of her religious conviction she would have undoubtedly lived and died the wife of a wealthy York merchant, unknown by history.

It is extremely difficult for those living in the secular twenty-first century society to understand the true depth of feeling that religion brought about in people in the past. It is also very difficult for many to understand how people living in Tudor times, both Catholic and Protestant alike, were willing to lay down their lives for their belief in God and their religion.

The obsession with Christianity goes back much further than the 16th century. In the period after it became the official religion of the Roman Empire, it was common for ordinary people to debate the true nature of Christ with such passion that they came to blows, often over their drinks, and sometimes ended up killing one another. One may speculate that this misguided intensity of feeling had little to do with Christ's message, or indeed his true nature as Son of God. The nearest analogy we can find today is perhaps the fervour that is felt over football and indeed sport as a whole. The passion which early Christians felt over defending Orthodoxy against Monophysitism was closely akin to supporters of Manchester United and Chelsea at a 'big match' which we often unfortunately see ends in fights and violence.

It has been said, very truly, that people in the past were much more concerned with the next world than this one, a position which is totally reversed in our own times. This was very understandable at the time in which Margaret lived. Life was relatively cheap and certainly very uncertain. Epidemic diseases such as plague and 'the sweat' could strike at any time and easily wipe out 15% to 20% of the population of a town or city at a stroke. Child mortality was very high and there was at least a 40% chance that a new-born child would never make adulthood. To live above fifty was a major achievement, especially among the poorer sections of society. Someone who achieved this age was seen as very ancient. Death was the constant companion of people in Tudor England. In these circumstances it was hardly surprising that they spent much of their time and effort in considering the nature of the world to come.

It is important to realise that religion formed a central core of people's lives at the time Margaret was born. For example, atheism or agnosticism were virtually unknown and were punishable by death. We might be tempted to think that people paid lip service to religion as a form of 'political correctness', however, this was certainly not the case. The depth of religious passion was absolutely genuine and heartfelt. The tragedy was that this fervour could lead to such deep intolerance and a parody of the Christian message to humanity.

The people of England in the century of Margaret's life suffered the most traumatic seesaw of religious belief that has ever been experienced in the long history of Christianity. There are very few Catholics alive today who would doubt that the Church was in a very serious state at the beginning of the sixteenth century. Corruption was rife and the sale of indulgences was only the tip of the iceberg. In the recent past there had been rival Popes, one at Avignon and the other in Rome, much to the confusion of the faithful. Furthermore, some of the medieval Popes, such as those of the Borgia family, could hardly be described as shining examples of sanctity or chastity.

Few would dispute that the Church was in very urgent need of reform and radical change. Indeed, the thinkers of the age such as St. Thomas More and Erasmus, were constantly urging reform and removal of corruption. There can be little doubt that this justified dissatisfaction with the Catholic Church brought about the Reformation. However, most Catholics argued then, and it would indeed be echoed by Catholics living now, that to demolish the entire structure of Christian belief and replace it with an untried alternative was to 'throw out the baby with the bath water'. It was to destroy the central pivot of Christian belief, which went back, unbroken, to the Apostles and indeed to Jesus Christ himself. This core was in no way affected by the undoubted abuses of power that the Catholic Church had fallen into. It was to destroy the sacred nature of worship, which had been refined over the centuries.

Even the most fervent Anglican could hardly dispute that Henry VIII's break with Rome was on purely political grounds, in his desire to have a son to follow him as King of England. Some Catholics might well wonder if it also had a great deal to do with Henry's sexual lusts for Anne Boleyn.

Nevertheless, the reasons for the move to the Protestant Church were of limited importance to ordinary people living at the time. They lived in a period when there was no freedom of expression and any irregular view was seen as a threat by the establishment and often termed high treason, for which there was only one penalty, death. They saw St. Thomas More, St. John Fisher, and others who refused to conform to the Protestant faith brutally executed. It was hardly surprising that the vast majority towed the party line and at least paid lip service to the 'new religion'.

Even so, there were strong regional divisions. The North remained fervently Catholic and this brought about The Pilgrimage of Grace which was brutally put down by Henry; in London and the South-East there was great enthusiasm for the new Protestant religion. They firmly set about dispensing with all things Catholic. This meant that people living in York and the surrounding district would have, in many cases, shown tacit compliance with the 'new religion', although most felt themselves to be spiritually and emotionally Catholics. It was likely that many had a strong feeling that things would stabilise and that the old, tried and trusted religion would return in due course.

The succession of Queen Mary in the year in which Margaret was probably born and the restoration of the Catholic faith would have been openly and genuinely welcomed by most living in the North. However, it created chaos in the South. The majority of the Protestant martyrs in the Marian period were in London and the South. Unfortunately Mary was out to seek revenge for the excesses of the Protestant attacks on Catholics. This led to hatred, bitterness and further division. Mary's marriage to Philip of Spain was viewed as a 'sell-out' to Europe and was very unpopular with most English people (including some Catholics), who had a deep-seated distrust of all things European.

Queen Elizabeth's return to Protestantism was a blow to those of Catholic thinking. Most of Margaret's short life was spent in Elizabeth's reign. To be fair to Queen Elizabeth she had no desire to create religious polarisation. She would have much preferred to have an accommodation with Catholics rather than to create martyrs. Unfortunately she was overtaken by events, in particular her rather unfortunate excommunication by the then Pope in 1570. It was, however, the intensity of certain Protestant feeling, verging on fanaticism and a desire to smash any opposition, which led to Margaret's horrific and untimely death at the Tollbooth on Ouse bridge in York in 1586. Much of this feeling stemmed from the new body of men and women who called themselves Puritans. These people believed it was 'the will of God' to tear limb from limb anyone who dissented from their belief in the nature of the Almighty.

This shows the extent of religious prejudice which then existed and this will perhaps partly explain why a pretty, vivacious and highly intelligent woman could be crushed to death simply because she would not conform to the established religious point of view.

Disease

In 1300 the population of England was estimated to be around six million, while in 1556 (only three years after Margaret's birth) it was estimated to be only 3.16m. The population of York in the early part of the fourteenth century was roughly 11,000, while in 1523 it was down to 8,000.

The major cause of this shrinking population was the virulent and much feared epidemics which swept the country periodically and often without much logic. As early as 1390 the bubonic plague killed 1,100 citizens of York and the following year raged with such deadly effect that over 12,000 people in England are thought to have died from it. Even today we often use the expression of 'avoiding something like the plague'. Clearly the horror of this disease is still evident in our subconscious.

Tudor England was just as subject to this terrible scourge as had been the case in medieval times. Hardly a year went past without an outbreak in some locality, while in London it was endemic. The fearsome disease was caused by the bite of an infected rat flea which led to swelling of the glands in the neck, armpit and groin. In later stages the symptoms varied. Some sufferers fell into a coma and behaved like sleepwalkers taking no account of anything. Others became violent and had to be forcibly restrained for, if they got free, they often ran off screaming as if pursued by the devil. In many cases these people did away with themselves. Occasionally there was no pain, and death was peaceful and 'natural'.

There was a 90% fatality rate and death normally took place within a week. The worst years of the sixteenth century for the bubonic plague were 1500/2, 1520, and 1535 to 1539. It appears to have killed particularly older children and teenagers and more men than women. It was an indelible part of life when Margaret lived and its appearance in a city such as York would put the entire population into panic and completely disrupted normal life.

Almost as deadly, and nearly as much feared as the plague, was the viral disease known as the 'English sweat'. The English sweating sickness, or *Sudor Anglicus,* was a devastating condition that showed no respect for age or social class. Among its most famous victims was Prince Arthur, the older brother of Henry VIII, who died from it when he was fifteen. A person could be healthy one day, fighting for breath the next and dead the following day. It was commonly described as 'merrie at dinner and dedde at supper'. It 'mended or ended' its victims in 24 hours. Like the plague it had peak epidemic years namely 1508, 1517, 1528 and 1551. In 1550 it struck York with great intensity. According to reports at the time, it reduced the population of the city by up to one third. Certainly in the Parish of St. Martin-cum-Gregory one third of the inhabitants died within two years.

Despite the terror in which 'the sweat' was held, it was sometimes less deadly than the plague and some did overcome it. Those who recovered or got the disease a second time learnt, by bitter experience, how to survive it. They found that keeping warm and avoiding food, coupled with a high intake of liquids, helped considerably.

Recent research has shown that a hantavirus, which originated from the droppings of mice and voles, may have caused 'the sweat'. One possible outbreak of this disease may have taken place in the south-west USA during 1993. At least 17 people died of a mystery virus rather similar to 'flu, but which developed much more quickly. The victim's lungs became flooded with fluid and most people who died did so within 72 hours of contracting the disease.

As if the plague and 'the sweat' were not enough to contend with, in 1557/8 a new virulent, mortal scourge emerged. This was christened 'the new sickness'. It was a burning hot fever and seems to have been akin to flu. However, unlike the plague, it followed no seasonal pattern. When it first appeared it led to death levels of up to four times above the previous annual average.

In 1557 it was recorded that:

> 'It (the new sickness) killed an exceeding great number of all sorts of men, but especially gentlemen and men of great wealth. So many husbandmen and labourers died that in some places the corn stood and shed on the ground for lack of workmen.'

York was hit by the 'new sickness' in 1558 and one report claimed that as much as 30% of the population died, although this may have been an exaggeration.

Apart from the ever-present dangers of the plague and other deadly diseases, public hygiene was non-existent. Most water supplies were severely infected, often by raw sewage. In York the source of much of the drinking water was the River Ouse, which was also the depository of the city's sewage. This was mitigated to some degree by the fact that in those days the Ouse was tidal.

It was common practice to empty the contents of chamber pots into the streets. This practice, which went back well into medieval times, gives us the word 'loo' for a toilet, for in Norman French times it was the custom to shout *'Gardez l'eau'* before emptying a chamber pot into the road. This led to grossly contaminated water and food and to the further spread of disease.

When Margaret lived in her home in the Shambles, the gutters of this street of the butchers literally ran with blood. Slaughtering and meat preparation was all done on the premises. There were no standards for food hygiene and the only method of preserving meat was salting it in barrels. It can be imagined what the smell must have been like and this was impossible to escape if one lived over the shop as Margaret and her husband John did.

Personal hygiene was very poor. Very few people could afford to bathe and it was common not to change one's clothes for months on end. As a result the people of the sixteenth century must have smelt to high heaven and the only means of masking this was by the lavish use of perfume.

Events in York and elsewhere during Margaret's short life

It gives some further perspective to Margaret to look at certain events, which took place when she was alive, some of which would have affected her closely.

1553: Mary, elder daughter of Henry VIII, became Queen and repealed the acts of her brother and father and restored the Catholic faith.

1555: One of the very few Protestant martyrs originating from the North was executed. He was Robert Farrar who was born at Edwood in Midgley. When a young man he became a Canon of the order of St. Austin. In 1533 he was appointed chaplain to Archbishop Cranmer and followed his patron's example and married. He was the last Prior of Nostell near Leeds. He surrendered his monastery in 1540 and was granted a pension of £100 a year (a huge sum at the time). He received this until he was made Bishop of St. David's in Wales. After Mary's accession he was examined for his faith and doctrine by the then Bishop of Winchester. He refused to renounce his 'heresies, schisms and errors', and was burnt at the stake in Camarthen.

1559: Soon after Elizabeth came to the throne, the church service was ordered to be performed in English and the Reformation continued after the short break during which England had returned to Catholicism.

1562: William Shakespeare was born at Stratford-on-Avon on 23 April.

1563: Queen Elizabeth decreed: 'Whoever by preaching, teaching, writing or open speech, doth notify that the eating of fish, or any forbearing of flesh, is in any manner a necessity for the saving of the soul of man, shall be punished as a spreader of false news.'

1564: A great flood occurred and the Ouse at York swept away two arches of the Ouse bridge with twelve houses that stood upon it. Several lives were lost.

1569: A rebellion broke out under the Earls of Northumberland and Westmoreland. This was with the objective of 'restoring the Catholic religion and to advance Mary, Queen of Scots to the throne of England'.

The Crown quickly put down this revolt. No fewer than 800 people suffered at the hands of the executioner. The Earl of Westmoreland escaped but Northumberland was taken. He died with great courage and dignity in 1572 (22 August) on the scaffold at the Pavement in York.

1573: The head of the Earl of Northumberland was stolen in the night from Micklegate Bar, York.

Also in this year 'a considerable earthquake' was felt in York.

A prison was built on Ouse Bridge, York. This was later to house Margaret while she was under sentence of death in 1586.

1577: Francis Drake discovered the coast of California.

1584: The Corpus Christi plays were ended in York. The ancient guilds or fraternities of Corpus Christi and the other free companies of York had performed these.

Childhood and Adolescence

Margaret was born around 1553 in a house in Davygate, York. This was the family home and lay in the Parish of St. Martin, Coney Street. This church still exists, although it was severely damaged by German bombing in World War II. It was rebuilt after the war.

Margaret's father was Thomas Middleton, a wax chandler by trade and a merchant of some wealth. Her mother was Jane, whose maiden name was Turner. Jane's father was Richard Turner, the landlord and owner of the Angel tavern, situated near Bootham Bar. Her parents were married in 1532. Margaret was one of four children: her brothers were Thomas and George and her sister, Alice.

It is worth remembering that Margaret grew up in considerable comfort compared with many of the poorer inhabitants of York. Thomas Middleton was a man of standing in York society and was, just before his death, made one of the two sheriffs of York. The Middleton household would have had servants to carry out the menial tasks. It is unlikely that food was ever short, which was certainly not the case with people lower down the social scale.

A wax chandler plied a trade which was in constant demand since candles were the only forms of lighting then available in houses. Furthermore, under the Catholic Church there was, as there is now, a continuous requirement for votive candles. These are burnt to the Blessed Virgin Mary and the saints for petitions. The advent of the Protestant Church, under which such practices were banned as 'popish idolatry', would have hit Thomas Middleton in his pocket.

It is worth remembering that in the first five years of her life Margaret would have been brought up a Catholic, under Queen Mary. It is certain she would have been given a Catholic baptism. Moreover, it is quite possible that some of her early memories of the Mass stayed with her. These could have been a factor in her later conversion to the Catholic faith. The old saying, 'Give me a child to the age of seven and it will be mine for life', may have partially applied to young Margaret Middleton.

Thomas Middleton was a churchwarden at St. Martin's Church and it is reasonable to assume that he supplied the church with its candles. When Elizabeth came to the throne the Middleton family accepted the legal requirement to attend a Protestant church and in so doing affirmed the Queen as head of the Church of England. However, the Middleton's family priest at St. Martin's did not. Father Henry More refused to conform to the new Protestant faith. He was deprived of his living and had all of his private property confiscated and was reduced to living in abject poverty.

Hardly surprisingly, little is known about Margaret's childhood. The general spirit of the time was, however, very different from modern standards in the upbringing of children. The old adage of 'spare the rod and spoil the child' was widely applied. Children in the mid-sixteenth century were brought up in awe of their parents and especially their father. Within Elizabethan households a father's word was law; not only could he freely beat his children, but his wife as well. When Margaret had her own children, she was a firm disciplinarian. There was a harsh attitude to children which modern thinking would find totally unacceptable.

People still accepted child mortality with complete resignation. Some writers have concluded that it was for this reason that people were much less attached to their children than we are today. Parents in Elizabethan times were, however, quick to get an ailing baby baptised', partly for spiritual reasons, but also to give the child an identity and a name.

At an early age children were made to undertake household tasks and to make themselves useful. It is probable that Margaret would have been made to help with the household chores when still a young child. This was seen as part of her training as a housewife. As she grew older she would have been taught to bake bread, brew ale and supervise the servants. However, she would not have been taught to read or write as this was not deemed to be essential for a woman. Children were encouraged to make their own games and pastimes. There was none of the structure, which applies today, in terms of using play as an aid to learning.

In 1564 Thomas Middleton was an ailing man suffering from acute gout. In that year he was appointed one of the two sheriffs of York, a singular honour and only exceeded by the prestigious office of Lord Mayor. Unfortunately Thomas was so ill that he was forced to take the oath of office in his bed. In 1567, when Margaret was 13 or 14, he died and was buried in his parish church of St. Martin's, Coney Street.

It was quite clear that he was a man of some wealth. Under his will Jane Middleton received 'the residue of all my lands and leases during her natural life'. This made her a very wealthy widow.

Margaret did well out of her father's will. She received the family home in Davygate after her mother's death: 'one house lying in Davygate within the City of York'. She also received an immediate bequest: 'also I give to the said Margaret one silver goblet and half a dozen silver spoons'. In fact, Margaret fared much better than her sister Alice, who only received 'a legacy of four marks in money'. The inheritance Margaret received was substantial for a teenager of her day.

Very shortly after Thomas's death Jane remarried. She was around 52 and almost certainly beyond childbearing age. It was common practice for a widow to remarry at the time. However, the time which elapsed after Thomas's death, only four months, was very short even by the standards of the sixteenth century. The man she married was Henry May. He was very much younger than her and was probably only in his twenties. In modern parlance we could say that Jane took for herself a 'toyboy'.

Henry was a very ambitious and calculating young man, with his eye on the main chance. He was not a local of York but originated from Hampshire and had settled in York where he established himself as an innkeeper. Undoubtedly he saw Jane as a passport to promotion within the City. It is also likely that he was attracted to her wealth.

Within a few months of his wedding to Jane, Henry May was given the post of chamberlain, which was seen as the first link in the chain for those destined for high office. Indeed, Henry was extremely successful in climbing the ladder and was Lord Mayor of York in 1586, the year Margaret was executed. His name is still inscribed on the ceremonial sword of the Lord Mayors of York. Henry was branded an adventurer by Father John Mush, who was Margaret's spiritual director and who had little reason to like this militant Protestant. One of Henry's first actions as head of his 'new' family was to turn the Davygate home into an inn. This would, of course, have increased his revenue. Even so, it is believed that this move was not unpopular with the family and was actively welcomed by Jane, who had been brought up as an innkeeper's daughter.

It is quite possible that Margaret may well have strongly resented Henry usurping her father's role. Especially since Henry might well have been only ten years older than herself. Furthermore, the relationship between children and step-parents is often fraught. Under the conventions of the times a father or stepfather's word was law. Margaret, it is known, could be headstrong and stubborn and wilful. Teenagers have always had a reputation for being rebellious and there is no reason to suppose this was not so in Tudor times. It is unlikely that Margaret's 'attitude problem' would have endeared her to Henry, who was only interested in his own advancement.

Henry May was a confirmed Protestant, mainly because he liked to swim with the tide of popular opinion, especially if it was likely to promote his cause. He would have been very likely to attack all things Catholic with the utmost vigour. He would have instilled into his wife and stepchildren a hatred of 'popery, the Mass and Catholic priests'. There can be no doubt that he would have been down like a ton of bricks on any remark that was not 'religiously correct'. It is possible that Margaret, through her resentment, rebelled against her stepfather's 'orthodox' religious views. This may well have been an unconscious step in her journey to joining the Catholic Church.

⌘

Marriage

Margaret married John Clitherow on 1 July 1571 at St. Martin's Church, Coney Street, York. The parish register shows the following entry:

John Clitherow and Margaret Middleton were married the first day of July in the yeare of our Lord (1571).

One may well speculate that Henry May was perhaps pleased and relieved to get Margaret off his hands and under the authority of a husband. He may have found her quite a handful, since we know she had considerable intelligence and a stubborn streak. These were unlikely to be attributes that a social climbing young man on the make would have valued in his stepdaughter. Needless to say, Henry married Margaret off with an eye to his benefit. He saw John Clitherow, who was a widower and considerably older than his new wife, as an ally in his rise up the social scale in York. In other words, a connection by marriage could benefit him, since John was a wealthy butcher from the Shambles and well thought of in York society.

John had been previously married to Matilda, daughter of Walter Mudd, butcher. She is believed to have died in 1570, possibly in childbirth, and to have left John with two infant sons, William and Thomas. William was subsequently ordained a Catholic priest in 1608, while Thomas became a draper, and was imprisoned for recusancy, dying in Hull jail. So Margaret took on two very young children from a former union from her first days of marriage.

The majority of marriages were arranged in Tudor times, certainly among members of the merchant class. One might think this led to unhappy, loveless marriages of convenience. Strangely, the system was not as bad as it might seem. Many marriages worked out well and it was frequent for couples to fall in love after they were married. In fact John and Margaret's marriage was extremely happy, and it was clear that both partners were in love with each other. It is quite possible that this love which Margaret had for John may well have been very important in her martyrdom, as later events will show.

John was the son of Richard Clitherow but his date of birth is not known. John became a bridgemaster in 1571 and subsequently a chamberlain, after which his advancement was curtailed by his wife's recusancy. He was a man of some wealth who always kept Margaret

Interior of St. Martin's church, Coney Street, York, as it is today.

and his children in comfort, a kind and considerate husband and father.

John Clitherow has had a very bad press. He has been depicted as a militant Protestant who abhorred Margaret's devotion to the Catholic faith, but circumstantial evidence points very clearly in the opposite direction. This view of John originates from Father John Mush's biography of Saint Margaret, written very shortly after her death. However, it must be realised that Father Mush may well have been a pragmatist and known that his document could easily fall into Protestant hands. If John Clitherow had been depicted as a Church Papist, and a sympathiser with the faith, his life could well have been in danger.

It has been claimed that John knew nothing of the fact that his home was used as a Mass centre in York. Although he did travel from home to his estate at Cornford, this is very unlikely, since he was an astute businessman and well aware of what was going on around him. It has also been said that he was unaware that a passage had been built from his house to the building next door to help Catholic priests escape in an emergency. This seems highly improbable. Anyone would be well aware if major building work was taking place in their home. It is very likely that John had to foot the bill.

Shortly before Margaret's arrest, their son, Henry, who was eleven or twelve, left York for the Continent to study for the Catholic priesthood. It stretches credulity to its uttermost limits to believe that John would meekly accept the disappearance of his son without any comment. The journey would have had to be paid for and young Henry would have had to have living expenses. It is only logical to assume that John was fully in the picture. Many of John's relatives were openly Catholic. His brother, William, entered Douai College in 1576 to train as a priest and was ordained six years later. One may speculate that this same William may have had a powerful influence on Margaret and could have been directly instrumental in her joining the Catholic Church.

Margaret brought up her children as Catholics. This led to her daughter, Anne, joining a convent at Louvain. She had a Catholic tutor for them, one Brian Stapleton, who is mentioned later in her story. It is extremely improbable that this could have happened without John's complete consent and knowledge. At that time a husband's word was absolute in law.

All these facts point to John being extremely sympathetic to Catholicism. It is almost certain he was a Church Papist, or 'Closet Catholic'. This meant that he attended the services at his parish church according to law, but secretly preferred the Catholic religion. Church Papists argued that the newly constituted Church of England's services were unobjectionable and claimed there was no need to listen to the sermon. Some even received communion, and reasoned that since it was not a true sacrament it was therefore harmless.

Recusants were obliged to pay a fine for non-attendance at their parish church. In John and Margaret's case they were obliged to pay an annual fine that would have been in the order of £4 to £5. This may sound a paltry sum today but it was substantial at that time. A master carpenter was then paid £5 10s (£5.50) a year. Even so, John paid this fine without any grumbles. If a male recusant persisted he could be banned from public office. A merchant could easily lose his business and be ruined. Customers were quite at liberty, under the law, to refuse to pay him if he was a Catholic. He would also lose custom from ardent Protestants.

It is very easy to judge John harshly for being unwilling to come out openly as a Catholic. There are contemporary records which show that many traders and merchants in York had Catholic wives, but were not themselves registered as recusants. Some genuine Protestants with Catholic wives were inclined to try to 'beat some sense' into their 'erring' womenfolk. It has been suggested that John was interested in his own advancement and in consequence sought public office. This premise does not stand up. John's advancement was completely curtailed by Margaret's activities. Is it not possible that in obtaining minor public office he was in a position to make conditions easier for Catholics in the City? John described the Mass as 'God's service': hardly the terminology of a confirmed Protestant who would have condemned all 'popery and idolatry as sinful and the work of the evil one'.

It is vital to give John his due credit since he has emerged as a rather obstructive and unsympathetic personality. He was probably very supportive to Margaret, and his family may well have been the catalyst to bring her into the Catholic faith. There is an often quoted story of John, under the influence of drink at a dinner party, deriding Catholics and claiming they were no better than anyone else. Margaret was significantly the only Catholic present. She burst into floods of tears and would not be comforted. While we will never know with certainty what lay behind this incident, is it not possible that it was staged-managed by the husband and wife?

Certainly, Margaret had the type of temperament that would have made her a superb actress. By showing his 'devotion' to Protestantism, for public consumption, John may have intended to get the authorities off his back. There can be little doubt that this incident would have been quickly reported to the agents of the Council of the North.

John was a kind, good and sympathetic husband. He clearly allowed Margaret much more freedom than was normal at the time. It was clear that Margaret adored him. The Clitherow marriage was in many ways much more akin to modern relationships in this century than to the narrow conformity of male-dominated Tudor England.

It has been claimed in a number of biographies of Saint Margaret Clitherow that John overlooked her Catholic activities because of his love for her. We might be tempted to think that religious differences between husband and wife were not of great importance in the sixteenth century. It is certainly true that in our own times there are many happy and successful marriages between men and women of different religious traditions. This probably reflects the ecumenical society we live in.

Things were dramatically different in less tolerant times. Perhaps the most likely analogy today would be in political terms. Most people would accept that if a right-wing Tory man was married to a woman with neo-Marxist sympathies the marriage would be likely to be very stormy. This is perhaps a fair comparison between a marriage between an avid Protestant and a devout Catholic in Tudor times.

On her marriage Margaret moved into the Shambles from her family's Davygate home. This street, where all the butchers of York were situated, is almost perfectly preserved to this day and is a major haunt of tourists visiting York. She would have found that there was a great deal to learn on becoming a butchers' wife: to know about cuts of meat and pricing and to man the shop in front of their home. She was marrying into a very clannish trade. Butchers were very inbred, and there may well have been some suspicion about this pretty 'outsider' who suddenly appeared in the Shambles.

Overall, the Clitherows were very comfortably off, and, in modern parlance, very middle class. They could easily have had a pleasant and uneventful life, slipping into contented old age, if Margaret had not had the call to become a Catholic.

The Bridge of Faith

It is not known when Margaret first decided that she wanted to become a Catholic. Nor is it known who prepared her for joining the Church, or where she was received.

Most converts to Catholicism discover, with time, that there are a combination of factors which bring conversion about. Indeed it is common for both friends and acquaintances to say, 'We could see you were moving in that direction.' Although some people decide to become Catholics because of one significant event, it is much more common for it to be a gradual process.

When Margaret was in her twenties many young and intelligent people were being attracted to the Catholic faith. It is possible this may have been an influence, a dangerous, but heady form of unconformity.

Many of John's relations had remained Catholic, in particular his brother, William Clitherow, who subsequently was ordained a priest. Although little is known about William, it is not unreasonable to suppose he may have been a regular visitor to the Shambles. It is easy to imagine a scene, in which Margaret, a young and attractive woman would be sitting eagerly with her brother-in-law discussing the subject of religion. William Clitherow had the fire and zeal to enter the priesthood at a time when a priest who was captured would be hanged, drawn and quartered in the Protestant realm of England. Ironically, it is possible that Henry May was an influence. His rigid hypocrisy could easily have alienated his stepdaughter from the Protestant faith. If this were the case, William would have had a willing convert.

Katherine Longley, in her excellent book, *St. Margaret Clitherow,* speculates that Margaret may well have been moved by the execution of the Earl of Northumberland in August, 1572. Certainly this took place near to Margaret's home and it is virtually impossible that she could have been unaware of it. The Earl died with a courage and dignity that affected all who saw his end. However, at the same time as the Earl's death over eight hundred people who had been involved in the revolt died at the executioner's hands. It is probable that John and Margaret knew some of these unfortunates. The courage many showed in dying for their faith touched the souls of many people.

It is worthwhile briefly outlining the problems, which Catholics faced in the early 1570s. When Henry VIII took control of the churches and monastic buildings of the Catholic Church, many felt it sounded the death knell of the Catholic faith in England. It was argued that, as it would be impossible for Catholics to hold services, their religion would die by default. It was evidently forgotten that the Mass is the very core of the Catholic faith and the venue where a Mass takes place is irrelevant. This applies today just as it did in Tudor times. One thinks for example of the huge open-air Masses celebrated by Pope John Paul II in the many countries he has visited.

The Protestants forced Catholicism back to the very roots of Christianity. When the early Church was a persecuted minority religion under the Roman Empire, worship often took place in Christians' homes. Similarly there was a refreshing return in Tudor England to the core values of Christian belief. Class distinctions became unimportant. The relationship between the clergy and the laity improved dramatically. There was no need for clergy to stand on their dignity or to have a 'them and us' relationship with the people. Every Catholic could be condemned as a traitor and imprisoned or, frequently, executed.

It must be said in all fairness to Queen Elizabeth that she was not essentially anti-Catholic in the first part of her reign. Indeed, she insisted that she did not want her Catholic subjects 'molested by an inquisition or examination of their consciences in causes of religion'. She vetoed a bill which made it illegal not to attend Anglican Communion services. She saw that martyrs would create polarisation and could destabilise her realm. However, Elizabeth was forced to bow to anti-Catholic pressure which was rife at the time, especially from the new religious sect of Puritans who were responsible for the worst excesses of the Reformation and did their best to make Christianity into a lack-lustre, sin-orientated religion.

The action of Pope Pius V (later Saint) in issuing his Bull, *Regnans in Excelsis*, was extremely unfortunate. In this the Pope declared Queen Elizabeth excommunicate and 'deprived her of her pretended title to the kingdom of England'. He further stated: 'and we do command and charge all and every nobleman, subjects and people and others aforesaid that they presume not to obey her or her orders, mandates, and laws'.

This made all Catholics traitors to the Crown of England. Most Catholics were more than willing to accept the Queen's temporal power, but could not agree to her being head of the Church. Most Catholics would indeed take this view today. This extremely ill-advised move by the Pope did much to increase hatred of Catholics and probably resulted in the death of many people.

Another action which scared and infuriated the Church of England was the arrival of Jesuit missions from the Continent. The Society of Jesus was formed after the Council of Trent, as a counter move to win

The front of St. Margaret Clitherow's house in the Shambles, York.

back Catholics after the Reformation. Jesuits were superbly trained, highly intelligent and very brave men. Their impact on Catholics and others they met was dramatic and long-lasting.

It is not known where Margaret was received into the Church. It is probable that it was in the home of a friend; some have speculated that this may have been the home of Dorothy Vavasour. It is certain that she would have been anointed with oil of chrism in exactly the same manner in which any convert is received today. Shortly after, she would have received the Host for the first time. There can be no doubt that she always remembered this moment of great joy and liberation during the rest of her life. Possibly Margaret experienced some limited hostility and suspicion when she joined the Church. Some 'cradle Catholics' may have had strong reservations about a convert. More important and relevant was the real fear that some converts might be spies planted by the Protestant Church. This was a major source of information to those who were determined to destroy Catholicism.

Margaret quickly overcame these hurdles and within a short time emerged as a natural leader within the Catholic community in York. Women were a key influence in the Catholic Church in Tudor England. This was quite extraordinary since in most matters women were seen as subordinate and treated as second class citizens.

There was a vital need in those times to have safe locations to hold Masses, and hear confessions. Women formed an important link, and in addition they offered comfort to the hard-pressed clergy who were understandably stressed with being hunted fugitives. When Margaret became a Catholic, the importance of women in the Church was hundreds of years ahead of its time.

In 1603 the Anglican Church ordered a census of recusants in each diocese. The results were very suspect since some Catholics pretended to be ill for long periods to avoid fines. Others became Church Papists and attended Anglican services, but did not accept the religion practised there.

In York Diocese there were listed 420 women and 300 men. This shows clearly that many men who were tradesmen and merchants almost certainly followed the old religion, but attended their parish church. If they had failed to do so they could have been ruined financially. At the same time they gave tacit approval to their wives' belonging to the Catholic religion and in most cases paid their fines without complaint.

The factors which brought Margaret into the Church will never be known. What is certain is that, in this event, the Holy Spirit lit a beacon that shone forth at the time and continues to illuminate us four hundred years afterwards.

Recusant

The fact that Margaret was a natural leader may well explain the reason for her frequent jail sentences, her arrest, mock trial and inhuman execution. Margaret became one of the leaders in a formidable group of Catholic women in York. She shared this role with Dorothy Vavasour, wife of Thomas Vavasour, a doctor, and one of the most eminent Catholic laymen in Yorkshire, if not in England. A relation by marriage of Dorothy's was a lady-in-waiting to Queen Elizabeth and came from Copmanthorpe near York. Dorothy maintained a leading Mass centre in York. As a result the authorities constantly shadowed her. This led to her being constantly in and out of jail. Her husband, Thomas, was as constant in his support of the Catholic cause. The Vavasours were extremely comfortably off and Thomas Vavasour could easily afford to take the consequences of his actions.

Dorothy Vavasour was a very close friend of Margaret, held in prison with her two daughters, Anne and Dorothy, when Margaret was there under sentence of death in 1586. She was, therefore, able to offer comfort and support at this critical time.

Another friend of Margaret's was Anne Lauder, wife of an attorney (lawyer). Anne was a flamboyant extrovert, who dressed with style and panache. She was also deeply committed to the Catholic cause. On one occasion she admonished the Lord Mayor of York in no uncertain terms. He in turn washed his hands of her and passed her on to the dreaded Council of the North. She suffered grievously for her belief and both she and her husband, John, were imprisoned in the infamous Blockhouse prison in Hull, before being transferred to prison in London where she died of disease in 1589.

Perhaps Margaret's closest friend was Anne Tesh. She is described in Mary Claridge's biography of the Saint as a 'kindred spirit'. Anne Tesh was often in jail with Margaret and this undoubtedly increased the bond between them. Anne Tesh's husband, Edward, described as 'a gentleman of Bishopfields', at first stood out with his wife against the Protestant religion but by 1583 had conformed to the Anglican Church.

Subsequently Anne was condemned to death for 'attempting to persuade to popery' (conversion to Catholicism), by the Council of the North. Her death was to be by burning at the stake. The Council, however, decided to cover its back by referring the decision to the

Queen herself. This was because Elizabeth had strong reservations about women suffering capital punishment. The Queen effectively reprieved Anne and replied to the Council: 'Your Lordships shall understand that Her Majesty is pleased that the execution of Tesh and Maskew (who was condemned with Anne) shall be forborne until you receive further directions in that behalf.' She was eventually released in 1603 after the death of Queen Elizabeth.

Margaret was certainly an established recusant by 1576. In the list of known Catholics for the parish of Christ Church in the City of York are listed:

> *Dorothy, wife of Doctor Thomas Vavasour; Frances wife of Geo Hall draper, Wm Hutton draper (who will come to church when excommunication on him is lifted) and his wife Mary; Janet wife of Percival Geldard butcher; Emot wife of Richd Halliday, girdler; Agnes wife of Jn Weddell junior butcher; Alice wife of Jn Cowling, pennyman; Jane West, servant of Geo Hall draper, and Anne Boyes, her fellow servant; Anne wife of Chris Kitchingman, carpenter;* <u>Margaret</u>, <u>wife of Jn Clitheroe</u>, <u>butcher</u>; *Janet wife of Wm Bachelor, butcher; Agnes wife of Jn Chambers, innkeeper (gone to Newcastle); Janet wife of Geo Smithes (says she now goes to church); Alice wife of Theo Rocke, butcher (says she now goes to church).*

It is plain from the above list that it spans the social spectrum from a doctor to several servants and emphasises the relatively classless nature of Tudor Catholicism at a time when social demarcations were normally very rigid. The list further shows the predominance of women as declared and open Catholics. Many of the husbands' trades were such that, if they had openly followed their wives' example, they would have faced financial ruin.

There was also a strong Catholic 'cell' among the butchers. Since they would all have been situated in the Shambles, it is likely that this street was constantly under surveillance by the York authorities. Margaret's first clash with the powers that be came in 1577. She was taken, with John, to account for her non-attendance at her parish church. John was held a few days, but Margaret was transferred to York Castle jail. Margaret was held until January, 1578, and then released on the basis of a bond that specified that she must return to jail in the April of that year. Her husband had to guarantee her 'good behaviour' and pay a fine of two shillings a week for each service she missed at her parish church. This constituted about £5-£6 per annum and represented a tidy sum in Tudor England.

Margaret's prison was a building adjoining Fishergate, surrounded on one side by the Ouse and on the other by the River Foss. The rivers frequently flooded some of the cells. These rivers were heavily polluted, mainly by raw sewage and many Catholics died from unspecified fevers and agues contracted in this foul place. Indeed, many of the other women recusants ended their days in this jail and their deaths were put down to 'natural causes'.

Life in prison must have been a severe culture shock to Margaret. She was completely deprived of her servants and as a member of the merchant class she had grown up with a retinue of servants from childhood.

There were, surprisingly, certain compensations. York jail was very lax and most items could be bought through the jailer. Catholics could mix freely together and even, when priests were held, celebrate the Mass. This must have had a remarkable effect of strengthening faith: quite the reverse intention of the authorities.

Being able to mix together fairly freely must have strengthened the bonds of friendship between Catholics that created links which did much to further the cause when they were out of jail. It must be added that not all jails were as accommodating as York was. The notorious Blockhouse jail in Hull made the lives of recusants a living hell.

During her various stays in prison Margaret learnt to read and write. This must have had a liberating effect on her and opened up new perspectives: the limitations on a highly intelligent woman who was illiterate must have been great.

Perhaps her greatest trauma was separation from her family and friends. This is still very much the lot of any prisoner of conscience. She may also have worried about the day-to-day running of John's business.

Between 1577 and the summer of 1584, Margaret was sent to prison three times. Her longest stay was about eighteen months.

What was Margaret Clitherow like as a person?

Much of the evidence regarding Margaret's character comes from her spiritual director (or as she would have called him, ghostly Father), Father John Mush. It is understandable that John Mush wanted to portray her sanctity but he wrote her biography very shortly after her death so had no opportunity to get a sense of balance, essential in considering anyone's personality. As a result, when one reads John Mush, or some of the later books based directly on his document, the impression is gained that Margaret was a rather wooden personality divorced from the real world. Even a little delving shows that nothing was further from the truth. Margaret emerges as a delightful person who was physically and mentally very attractive.

Physically Margaret was described during her life as 'comely' and was undoubtedly a highly attractive woman. She had bright, brown hair. There is a tradition that she was of small stature. Certainly the well-attested relic of her hand, at the Bar Convent, York, would indicate a petite woman. It must also be remembered that most people in the sixteenth century were much smaller than people of today. This was due to a large degree to their diet. A woman today of 5ft 8in is considered a normal height. In Tudor times she would have been thought exceptionally tall.

In terms of personality Margaret was described by those who knew her as clear-headed, strong-willed, and warm-hearted. It is known she had a quick temper and could be stubborn. She was also described as 'merry, smiling and brave' and could be very witty. One can deduce that she had great self-confidence and was a highly intelligent person. She could undoubtedly hold her own in conversation, or discussion.

Margaret certainly did not see herself as a saint. She was well aware that she had human failings and said:

> 'God knoweth I am far off that which I should be; I am clogged with imperfections. But with God's Grace I never intend willingly to sin against God's will, though it were to be to gain the whole world or save my temporal life.'

These words proved to be prophetic in view of her frightful martyrdom.

Margaret was a person others turned to if they were in trouble. She was a true friend in need and extremely popular among both Protestants and Catholics. It seems highly probable that many of her neighbours, who were not Catholic, were well aware of her activities and turned a blind eye to them. Certainly they did not feel inclined to 'shop' her to the authorities.

She was a kind and loving mother, both to her own children and to the step-sons John brought with him to their marriage. It would be wrong, though, to see her as a sentimental mother. She could be very strict and had no compunction in using the whip if a child was disobedient. This may seem harsh by present-day standards, but it was the norm in her time. She educated her children as Catholics and insisted they spent considerable time in prayer.

Margaret knew how to manage her servants and was obviously liked and respected by them. But she was not soft and would admonish them sharply if they were at fault. She led by example and would carry out the menial tasks herself, such as sweeping the house, washing the dishes and even emptying the chamber pots, thus leaving her maids free to do more congenial tasks such as cooking. She said, in this context,

> 'God forbid that I should will any to do that thing in my house, which I would not first willingly do myself.'

She added:

> 'They that are not willing to do such base things, have little regard of well doing or knowledge of themselves.'

The relationship with her servants was very good, and their liking and respect helped to protect her from enquiry. It would be stretching credulity too far to believe they did not know of her sheltering priests or holding Masses in her home. Nevertheless, none betrayed her activities.

Margaret had considerable inner tranquillity. This must have given her great comfort, especially when she was under great stress during the period of her mock trial and before her execution. She demonstrated an incredible degree of self-confidence during her trial, standing up to her judges without any apparent fear. Those who sat in judgement on her at the Guildhall, York, would have been determined to break this 'simple housewife'. They singularly failed in their objective.

Perhaps her most remarkable attribute was that, despite her compassion and humanity, she had a vein of pure steel in her soul. This emerged very powerfully in her last days on earth. She managed, very successfully, to rebuff all attempts to make her change her mind and resisted pressure that would have made most people crack, emerging unscathed.

Margaret was a realist. As the end approached she had no delusions about her fate. Father John Mush warned her that her actions could easily lead to the rope. Margaret's reply was characteristic:

> 'God's will be done, but I am not worthy of that honour.'

She disagreed with John on the accumulation of wealth. Margaret showed that she believed that riches and its trappings were secondary to her relationship to God. John, on the other hand, was in many ways a typical businessman and he attached great store to his social status. John's money, nevertheless, had a considerable effect on Margaret's ability to carry out her work for the Catholic cause. Had she been living in abject poverty, it is very unlikely that she would have made such a positive contribution.

Margaret was certainly no prude. This was typical of the age she lived in, which was basic and earthy. She could express herself very graphically. For example, when, she mentioned her very natural fear of death she said:

> 'I confess that death is fearful. I intend to give up my life
> for the (Catholic) faith as willingly as I would give my
> children my paps (breasts) to suckle.'

One may well speculate that this type of expression would have had our Victorian ancestors reaching for the smelling salts. The Elizabethan age, for all its faults of religious intolerance, could not be accused of hypocrisy in matters of a sexual nature.

Her tastes were simple. She disliked excess and refused to go to the many feasts and banquets to which John was invited. Her favourite food was rye bread, milk, pottage and butter. Rye bread was the food of the poor, and Margaret could certainly have afforded a more expensive alternative.

Her spiritual life was central to her being. She prayed at least one to two hours a day, meditating on Christ's passion. She would pray with her children for an hour in the evening. She went to confession twice a week, and fasted on Monday, Wednesday and Saturday. On Friday she took only one meal, of bread and water. When she received the Host in the Mass she often wept. She had a firm and constant purpose not to do anything that she saw as 'offensive to Almighty God', although she would freely admit that she often failed.

When the martyrdoms began in York, she would slip out at night to the Knavesmire, where the executions took place. In doing this she had to bribe the night watchman at Micklegate Bar, clearly a very dangerous action and one that would bring her under scrutiny. On reaching the scaffold she would contemplate the suffering of the Catholic priests and lay people who had died for the Catholic faith.

We may well see this action as somewhat macabre by modern standards. Elizabethans, however, were much closer to violent death than we are. It is unlikely that anyone at the time would have seen this behaviour as in any way odd.

After learning to read and write in prison she began to read Thomas à Kempis's *Imitation of Christ* and found great strength from this book. It was banned and she received a copy smuggled in from Rheims.

From this picture of Margaret we can see a deeply spiritual woman. She was also extremely human, and was not without her faults. Margaret would have been horrified if she had been portrayed as a plaster saint. She had a humanity and vitality as well as supreme courage which reaches out to people living under totally different social and political conditions four hundred years later.

The beginning of the end

In 1584 Margaret arranged for her son, Henry, then aged twelve, to go to Rheims to be educated as a Catholic priest. It seems inconceivable that John Clitherow was not in agreement with this. John Mush claims that he was kept in the dark about this journey and the intention to make Henry a priest. This seems to run contrary to human nature. Any father, then or now, would want to know in very definite terms where his son had gone. John held the family purse strings and the journey would not have financed itself.

If one accepts that John was very much involved and in agreement with young Henry's trip to the Continent, one can also assume that he was very much in the picture on most of Margaret's actions to promote the Catholic Church in York. This would have put him in a position where he would certainly have faced a treason charge himself, and a possible death penalty. This gives an additional dimension to Margaret's martyrdom. She was not only dying for the Catholic Church but to protect the man she loved.

Margaret was sailing very close to the wind, and she was well aware of her danger. The absence of her son was very soon noticed. News of this spread like wildfire in the village-like atmosphere of York. It would be a major scandal among other merchants and those further down the social scale such as servants. Consequently, those people in York such as the sheriffs, who were concerned with monitoring the activities of Catholics, would have quickly been aware of this news. They in turn would have speedily passed on this information to the Council of the North, which was employed to implement the Queen's laws in northern parts.

Margaret had been under surveillance for some time, and they now saw an opportunity to rid themselves of a 'hated papist', who was also a leader of the many Catholic women in York. In 1585, new anti-Catholic legislation was introduced under which the penalties for 'harbouring or maintaining a Catholic priest' were increased and often included death. There were also laws introduced regarding English students who had gone abroad to seminaries. They were obliged to return in six months or their parents would face a fine of £100, a vast sum at the time equivalent to tens of thousands of pounds today. There is little doubt that if John had been forced to pay it he would have been bankrupted.

Another feature in Margaret's undoing was the election of a militantly Protestant Lord Mayor of York, Andrew Trewe. Some previous Lord Mayors had turned a blind eye to some aspects of

Catholicism. However, Lord Mayor Trewe wanted to dispose of 'dissident elements'.

In addition, Henry May, Margaret's social-climbing stepfather, also featured. In 1585 Margaret's mother, Jane, died. Under the terms of Thomas Middleton's will the family home in Davygate looked as if it would revert to Margaret. This must have put Henry into a flat spin. Not only could he lose out on this property, but also Margaret's activities could deprive him of his ultimate goal of being Lord Mayor. He believed that he could scare his stepdaughter into submission and make her renounce her Catholic faith. Clearly Henry made a serious error of judgement and did not appreciate the nature of the woman he was up against.

In 1586 Henry May achieved his ultimate aim and was elected Lord Mayor. It was also the year in which he had to contend with the unedifying spectacle of his stepdaughter's arrest, imprisonment and execution. Henry's calculation that he could force her into apostatising had gone badly wrong. He found himself in a very difficult, and embarrassing position: if he had any compassion he would also have found it very traumatic.

Margaret was getting into an increasingly vulnerable position. Hatred of Catholics was growing extremely fast and the Puritans were rapidly dominating the religious world. These saw Catholic worship as idolatrous and evil. In the seventeenth century they abolished Christmas, banning all frivolity or enjoyment, claiming it was sinful. They desecrated many beautiful parish churches, breaking medieval stained glass, smashing statues, and ripping out the monumental brasses all for the 'greater glory of God'. To the Puritans, Margaret's religion would have been anathema. However, they would have disliked her character as well, considering her openness and *joie de vivre* intensely worrying.

To the Puritans there was only one method of countering a person of Margaret's personality and strength, and that was to eliminate them. This is doubtless what they decided to do and the die was cast towards her martyrdom. Priests were being executed all over England. Certainly Margaret knew well many of those who were killed at the Knavesmire. Often they suffered the horrendous death of hanging, drawing and quartering. In this the victim was hanged by the neck, and, while still alive, cut down and disembowelled in front of the assembled crowd. Finally their body was cut into portions.

One priest who died about this time with exceptional courage on the Knavesmire in York was Father Thomas Nutter. His demeanour was so unusual in that he 'welcomed death as a spiritual marriage', and spectators were amazed at his eagerness to be united with God. As a result, rather unfairly, the term 'nutter' or 'nutcase' has passed into English as someone with a serious mental health problem.

Arrest

In the afternoon of Thursday, 10 March, 1586, the two sheriffs of York, Roland Fawcett and William Gibson, and their retinue raided Margaret and John's home in the Shambles. There had been warning of this happening, since, the day before, John had been summoned before the Council of the North to explain the absence of his son, Henry. John had attended, but the first time he went the Council was too occupied with other business to see him. He was ordered to return later.

Margaret was clearly alarmed by the situation and said:

> 'Now that they have him, they will make my house to be searched.'

It is highly likely that she hid any items that might incriminate her.

When the raid came Margaret was about her household duties. In the next house was a Catholic priest, but word quickly reached him and he escaped safely. In the attic the Catholic tutor, Brian Stapleton, was teaching Margaret's children and those of friends and neighbours. Suddenly 'a ruffian bearing a sword and buckler' opened the door of the schoolroom. He obviously thought that Stapleton was a priest and alerted his companions. Brian Stapleton did not understand the situation and believed the man was a friend and was about to call him in. Quickly realising his mistake, and he escaped through the passage built to the next door house, got away. The sheriff's posse came up the stairs to the schoolroom in great haste, and finding that 'the bird had flown' were furious. They apparently 'raged like madmen'.

Margaret was arrested and taken. All the children and house servants were held in custody. The men then searched the house very carefully but found nothing. This bears out the premise that Margaret had hidden the most damning evidence the day before.

The sheriffs were quick to interrogate the children. The youngest of Margaret's children was only ten. None of her children broke. The interrogators, however, found a weak link in a boy who had recently come from Flanders and was known as 'the Flemish boy'. He was only around ten to twelve years old himself but was stripped naked and threatened with a beating if he did not give them the information they wanted in a move reminiscent of the Nazi death camps. This boy quickly gave in and took his captors to the priest's room. There they found vestments, banned books and items used in Catholic worship. The children and servants were scattered around the various jails in York.

Margaret was clearly their 'star prisoner' and she was taken at once to appear before the Council at King's Manor. She kept her composure despite their 'cruel threats and railing'. This was the first time she had come face to face with the Council of the North. Her self-confidence and calmness was incredible considering the pressure put on her from the very start.

She had no opportunity to prepare any defence, nor was she given access to a lawyer. Indeed, in those times defendants were completely on their own. Certainly the style of justice given out in Tudor times was very similar to that which existed in Stalin's Russia.

John was kept overnight, completely separated from his wife. Margaret was then transferred to the Castle prison. When she arrived some Catholic prisoners noticed that she was soaked to the skin and had to borrow dry clothes. It is believed that the sheriffs tried to break her spirit by using the ducking stool, which stood by the river Ouse.

The unfortunate Flemish boy supplied a list of names of people he remembered at the Masses at Margaret's house. This included her special friend, Anne Tesh, who was promptly arrested and held in prison. The boy accused her of 'harbouring and maintaining divers priests'. Specifically mentioned were Father Francis Ingleby and her spiritual director, Father John Mush. This news was passed on to her in prison, and she was further told that this was a capital offence.

Margaret's reaction was perhaps surprising as she said to the messenger:

> 'I would I had some good thing to give you for this good news. Hold take this fig, for I have nothing better.'

Margaret only saw her husband once in jail. No record of their conversation exists. However, it is known that the jailer was present.

Margaret made herself ready to be called in front of her judges. All contemporary reports indicate that she was self-controlled even 'merry'. Before she was summoned before the Council she jokingly made the sign of a gallows to other Catholic prisoners to indicate her likely fate. She was under no illusions that the Council was after her blood and whatever emerged at the trial would not alter the outcome in any way.

'Justice'

She was held over the weekend and on the evening of Monday, 14 March, 1586, she was taken for a preliminary hearing to the Guildhall in York. It is important to understand that in Tudor times most people were ignorant of the law but still had to carry out their own defence, frequently without time for preparation. Trials such as those of Saint Thomas More were exceptional in that he was a leading lawyer of his time and probably knew the law better than his opponents. Tudor justice was probably very similar to the worst form of totalitarian state in the modern world. All the cards were weighted in favour of the state and had little to do with defending the rights of the accused.

Margaret was well aware of her vulnerable position, and had few delusions as to the outcome. She knew that the Council had already decided on her death and to make an example of her. Before her arrest she had frequently appeared before the local justices and had been sent to prison. Now, however, she was up against a much more formidable team: Lord Evers, the Vice President of the Council of the North, as well as judges, Clench and Rodes. There were also in attendance legal counsellors, Meers and Hurlestone. Present, too was the Secretary of the Council, Henry Cheke. To overawe the prisoner even further was none other than her stepfather, Henry May, in his capacity as Lord Mayor, with all the aldermen of the City.

Despite Margaret's apparent calmness, one must wonder if she did not have a twinge of panic when she saw what she was up against.

To start the proceedings a criminal indictment was read out her, which was phrased in such a manner as to further overawe a prisoner.

Judge Clench opened the case for the crown. He said:

> 'Margaret Clitherow, how say you? Are you guilty of the indictment or no.'

Margaret replied quite calmly:

> 'I know of no offence whereof I should confess myself guilty.'

Clench then brought forward the main charge, one for which the penalty was death:

'Yes, you have harboured and maintained Jesuits and priests, enemies of Her Majesty.'

Margaret was quick to deny that she had ever harboured any one who was an enemy of the crown. The judge then came to the question of Margaret's trial and asked her:

'How will you be tried?'

The normal answer was for a prisoner to give was 'by God and the country'. However, Margaret denied any guilt and therefore disputed that she should be tried. She said:

'Having no offence, I need no trial.'

Clench and his fellow judge, Rodes, were nonplussed. Here was a prisoner attempting to dictate the limits of the law. This was unheard of and clearly the court's authority had to be established. They told her clearly that she had offended against the statutes of the law and must face trial. Margaret responded:

'If you say I have offended then I must be tried. I will be tried by none but God, and your consciences.'

Clench was now beginning to lose patience with this stubborn and headstrong woman. He told her quite categorically:

'You must be tried by the country.'

Margaret then repeated her wish to be tried:

'By none but God and your consciences.'

Here was total stalemate which her judges resolved in a strange manner. Indeed, they may even have wished to introduce a little light relief into the proceedings. They brought out the vestments and other items used in Catholic worship which they had taken from her home including chalices and religious pictures. They dressed up 'two lewd fellows' in vestments, who then paraded around the judges and Margaret, holding up unconsecrated Hosts. This, one may assume, was greeted by howls of laughter from the assembled company.

The judges attempted to humiliate her by saying:

'Behold thy gods in which thou believist!'

They then asked her pointedly:

'How do you like those vestments?'

Margaret replied:

'I like them well, if they were on the backs of they that know to use them in God's honour.'

It was clear that Clench believed that he could quickly gauge the level of Margaret's religious belief, and he started on a new tack:

He asked her pointedly:

'In whom believe you?'

She replied:

'I believe in God'

Clench followed up his attack:

'In what God?'

Margaret answered without any hesitation:

'I believe in God the Father, in God the Son, and God the Holy Ghost; in these three persons and one God I fully believe, and by the passion, death and merits of Christ Jesu, I will be saved.'

Clench realised he was not likely to demolish her faith and was forced to say:

'You say well.'

Having failed in his attack Clench now reverted to the question of her trial. Both he and Rodes said:

'Margaret Clitherow, how say you yet? Are you content to be tried by God and the country?'

She refused this and Clench then pointed out that a refusal to be tried by the country would establish her guilt, and would make her responsible for her own death. He also hinted that it was unlikely that she would be condemned solely on the evidence of a young child.

Margaret was still unswayed. The judges then attempted to establish whether John Clitherow knew of her activities.

They asked pointedly:

'Was your husband privy to your doings in keeping priests?'

Margaret had clearly been expecting this attack and denied her husband's involvement. She evaded the question and this appeared to eliminate John from the proceedings. Clench's patience was now at breaking point and he said quite brutally:

'We must proceed by law against you, which will condemn you to a sharp death for want of a trial.'

Margaret replied:

'God's will be done: I thank God I may suffer any death for this good cause.'

It was clear that the judges had thought that Margaret would be a pushover and they now realised that they had not come out well.

They began a vituperative attack on the Catholic Church and its priests. Hurlestone came out with a quite ridiculous and slanderous statement. He claimed.

> 'It is not for religion that thou harbourest priests, but for whoredom.'

This showed the depths of depravity that the accusers were willing to sink to in their attempt to prove her guilty.

The judges then rose for the night without resolving her trial.

Margaret was taken to the prison on Ouse bridge, where she had an opportunity to consider her position. She must have thought about John's complicity and realised that a full trial would undoubtedly have exposed this. Furthermore, she would have worried that her friends and relations could have been implicated. Indeed, many people might have suffered the death penalty as well as her.

The following day she was taken before her judges again, early, indeed at 8 am. Clench came straight to the point. He said if she went to trial she had little to fear, as the chief witness would be a young child.

Margaret replied with spirit:

> 'I think if you have no witness against me but children, which with apple and a rod you may make to say what you will.'

Clench now used more determined tactics:

> 'It is plain that you had priests in your house, by these things that were found.'

Margaret pinned her colours to the mast and said:

> 'As for good Catholic priests, I know no cause why I should refuse them as long as I live; they come only to do good to me and others.'

This brought an eruption of fury from the bench:

> 'They are all traitors, rascals, and deceivers of the Queen's subjects.'

Margaret replied with equal spirit:

> 'God forgive you. You would not say so if you knew them.'

She went further:

> 'I know them to be virtuous men, sent by God to save our souls.'

Clench then returned to the question of her trial:

'Will you put yourself to the country yea or no?'

Margaret then uttered the words which almost certainly sealed her fate:

'I refer my cause only to God and your consciences. Do what you think good.'

The judge then told her directly that if she would not yield he must, reluctantly, pass sentence on her. However, he also pointed out:

'Mercy lieth in our hands, in the country's also, if you put your trial to them.'

Margaret could not be moved and Clench was obviously reluctant to condemn this beautiful and self-confident young woman. Rodes, his fellow judge, was less merciful. He became exasperated and burst out:

'Why stand we all this day about this naughty wilful woman? Let us despatch her.'

Clench was then forced to pronounce the dreadful sentence of *peine forte et dure:*

'You must return whence you came, and there in the lowest part of the prison, be stripped naked, laid down, your back upon the ground, and as much weight laid upon you as you are able to bear and continue three days without meat or drink, except a little barley bread and puddle water, and the third day be pressed to death, your hands and feet tied to posts, and a sharp stone under your back.'

It was plain that Margaret did not know until the sentence what her fate would be. She was shamed by the fact she must die naked. However, her response was quite heroic:

'If this judgement be according to your conscience, I pray God send you better judgement before him. I thank you heartily for this.'

Even after sentence, Clench was clearly unhappy and still urged her to go to trial. He begged her to consider her family and the effect on them. Margaret knew the die was cast and said:

'I would to God that my husband and children might suffer with me for so good a cause.'

Clench made a final appeal to her to be tried by the country. She rejected this:

'I am not worthy of good a death as this: I have deserved death for mine offences to God, but not anything I am accused of.'

She was pinioned and taken under armed guard to her prison on the bridge, to await her death after this show of so-called 'English justice'.

Preparing for death

A tradition has grown that Margaret Clitherow was desperate to die for the Catholic cause. This has led to some allegations that she committed suicide through her actions rather than being a victim of religious oppression. These views were current around the time of her death, and, indeed, originated from her stepfather, Henry May. He must have found the whole position rather embarrassing in view of his status. He, therefore, had to find a let-out to distance himself from Margaret's death, and any effects it could have on him. This shows his depravity and self-centredness. Yet the view that Margaret killed herself is still occasionally voiced today.

It is essential to nail this lie before considering the Saint's last days on earth. If one accepts that she was protecting her husband, relations and friends, then she was following the teaching of Jesus Christ when he said:

> 'Greater love has no man than that he lay down his life
> for his friends.'

In dying for her religion she was following the precedent of St. Thomas More, and St. John Fisher, as well as many Catholic priests and laymen. Similarly, the Anglican bishops, Latimer, Ridley and Cranmer, died in Oxford for their belief in Almighty God and the Protestant Church.

There is no doubt that Margaret was scared by the prospect of death, as is any normal person. Equally there is no question that she was 'half in love with easeful death'.

The following statements by her made when she was under death sentence make this quite plain:

> 'I am according to the Queen's majesty's laws judged to
> die, and while my spirit is willing, though my flesh may
> repine.'
> 'My cause is God's and it is a comfort to die in his quarrel;
> flesh is frail, but I trust in my Lord Jesu that he will give
> me the strength to bare all troubles and torments which
> will be laid upon me for his sake.'
> 'I shall die on Friday next. I now feel the frailty of mine
> own flesh which trembleth at the news, although my spirit
> greatly rejoiceth.'

These are hardly the thoughts of a woman determined on her own self destruction.

Within a short time of the verdict there was a full-scale scandal in York. Firstly, Margaret was extremely popular with Catholics and Protestants alike. Moreover, she was a woman of standing in the City, with a husband who was a prominent merchant. She was also stepdaughter of the Lord Mayor. The verdict was uncomfortably close to many of the citizens of sixteenth-century York. Many were eager to find a method of deferring her execution. Probably the most obvious method was to claim she was pregnant. No woman could be executed by law, until after the birth of her baby, since this destroyed an innocent life.

A rumour that Margaret was with child sped around like wildfire through the village-like environment of York. It was not long, as her friends intended, that this came to the ears of her judges. Judge Clench, who was certainly unhappy about her sentence, seized on this and said:

'She may not be executed for they say she is with child.'

The other judges were less merciful and acting under the Council's instructions were determined to rid themselves of Margaret. However, Clench, acting on his own, decided to get some women friends to approach Margaret and find out if she was pregnant. When this delegation visited Margaret, she was ambiguous, and said she was uncertain if she was with child. She said if she was pregnant that it was at a very early stage. Clench was keen to give her the benefit of the doubt and to grant an 'order of venter', which would delay execution for at least 20 weeks. However, his colleagues overruled him.

When John heard the verdict he went berserk. He wept so violently that this caused him to have a major nosebleed. He shouted out in total despair:

'Alas, they will kill my wife. Let them take all I have to save her *for she is the best wife in all England and the best Catholic also.*'

It is not hard to realise John's trauma and his love for Margaret shone through. In saying she was the best Catholic in England, hardly the sentiment of a militant Protestant, we may speculate he came very close to nailing his true colours to the mast.

Even when she was condemned, she was still questioned by members of the Council of the North who wanted her to renounce her faith and hence win a propaganda victory. They also tried to pump her for information with a view to implicating other Catholics and to find out details of the whereabouts of Catholic priests.

She was also pestered by so-called Puritan Divines, especially by one Edmund Bunney. Bunney delighted in taunting Catholic priests on the scaffold. Very wisely, Margaret kept him at arm's length. He tried to trick her as a means of shaking her faith, obviously thinking he was up against a simple uneducated housewife; he soon discovered his error. Margaret politely but firmly refused to discuss her doctrine of faith with this man. On one occasion he visited her with Robert Pease and a well-known Irish Puritan, James Cotrell. These three men attempted to break her belief.

She was much more receptive to Giles Wiggington, who had tried to intervene on her behalf when she was in front of her judges. She saw him as a good and honest man whose religious belief differed from her own. While she could never accept his beliefs she knew him as a person of integrity and compassion and was much more willing to discuss her spiritual beliefs with him. In fact, Wiggington virtually begged her to attend one sermon in the Anglican Church to save her life.

Margaret said:

'I will with all my heart hear a sermon.'

This made Wigginton think he was making progress. However, she then qualified it by saying:

'I pray you understand me. I mind not if I may have a Catholic priest or preacher, but come to your sermons I will never.'

Eventually Giles Wigginton gave up the struggle of shifting her opinion.

Finally Henry May, her stepfather, went to her and begged her on his knees to go against her conscience. He said if she did this that he would use his influence to get her a pardon. Margaret, one can guess, had her liking for Henry well under control, and saw him for the grasping opportunist that he was. She refused him. He then spread the lie that she was determined to commit suicide, a slur that followed her after her death. May then showed his complete ignominy when he spread rumours that she was an immoral woman. This action came from a man who was in law her father. Henry May can only be described as depraved and perverted.

Margaret surely knew her death was very close and brought her soul into balance with God, to face her awful ordeal. The tactics used by the Council of the North were similar to the worst sort of dictatorship. In a final attempt to break her will, they claimed she had slept with Catholic priests and cheated on John. She was told the Flemish boy was their informant. She dismissed these foul lies with the contempt they deserved and said:

> 'If I have offended my husband in anything but my
> conscience, I ask God's forgiveness . . . I trust my husband
> will not accuse me that I have offended him in any time,
> unless in such small matters that are commonly incident
> to man and wife.'

In her last days the full power of Margaret's personality shines forth.
It is well known that she was a woman of great compassion, but she
had also a vein of granite in her soul. She could resist every attempt to
break her spirit, and left her accusers in confusion. Certainly the
Council of the North had its twentieth-century equivalent, namely
the Gestapo of Hitler's Third Reich.

Ouse Bridge, York, in Elizabethan times. Margaret was held and executed here.

The Martyr's Crown

It became apparent during the second week of her captivity that the end was rapidly approaching. When the weekend came John was told by the Council of the North to 'depart the city for five days'.

On Tuesday evening, 22 March, 1586, the two sheriffs, Fawcett and Gibson, came and told her she was to die on Friday.

It is interesting that Margaret's execution was in private. Most of the executions of whatever form were in public. This was to keep the masses in awe as well as to provide a vicarious amusement to the mob. Certainly it was common practice for Catholics to be executed in public as no doubt a 'lesson to all those who dissented from the established church'. Why then was Margaret made an exception? May we not speculate that with her popularity and the strength of feeling against her death in York a riot might have been possible if she had been killed on the Knavesmire?

It is believed that Margaret's great friend, Dorothy Vavasour, was in prison with her and was able to comfort Margaret in her plight. Here we see Margaret at her most vulnerable, a terrified human being facing the unknown. She said very understandably:

> 'Now I feel the frailty of mine own flesh, which trembleth
> at the news.'

She fell to her knees and prayed to Almighty God for strength to face her terrible ordeal. Hardly the behaviour of a 'suicide', as Henry May was quick to tell all the people he knew. After her date of execution had been told her, Margaret took no further food. She occupied herself in making a shift that she would wear on the coming Friday. Although her sentence had decreed that she must be stripped naked, perhaps she expected some latitude on this matter. Into this shift she sewed tapes so that her hands could be bound and that she might die with her arms outstretched, in the attitude of Jesus on the Cross. On the surface this might appear slightly morbid, even helping her executioners. Her motive may have been that she did not want her body to contort in her death throws, but to die with the utmost dignity. We shall never know this for certain.

The day before her death she was transferred to the parlour of Mr. and Mrs. Yoward. They were Protestants, who were possibly in prison for debt. However, a bond grew up between Mrs. Yoward and Margaret, despite their different traditions. On the evening of her last night on earth Margaret said to Mrs. Yoward:

> 'I would gladly have the maids (possibly Mrs. Vavasour's
> two daughters) bear me company this night, not for fear
> of death, but for my comfort, but the flesh is frail.'

Mrs. Yoward told her that the jailer had left and they were locked in for the night. Out of compassion Mrs. Yoward stayed with Margaret, and at midnight, the start of the day of her death, she knelt in prayer until 3 am. After this she went and lay on the floor in front of the fireplace for about fifteen minutes. Was she possibly rehearsing the events, which were to come?

Margaret then went to bed, (although one must wonder if she slept) until six in the morning, when she got up and prepared herself for the sheriffs' arrival. She asked Mrs. Yoward to come to her execution, probably because she wanted a friend close to her. Mrs. Yoward refused. She said she had no wish 'To see such a cruel death for all of York.'

She, did, however, suggest to Margaret that she could get some of her friends to place the weights on her so that 'You may be quickly dispatched from your pain.'

Margaret immediately vetoed this since she did not want 'Any to be guilty of my death and blood.'

At 8 am the two sheriffs arrived with their retinue to take her to the place of execution. She went with them, bare-headed and bare-legged, carrying her shift. She simply had to cross the street to the Tollbooth that stood at the far end of Micklegate at the end of the bridge. Since the Old Ouse Bridge was demolished in the nineteenth century, we can only speculate about the position of the Tollbooth. It is likely that the nearest point today would be the steps leading to Queen's Staith. The Tollbooth was normally used to get tolls from people visiting York from the country. By a strange irony John had been a bridgemaster in the past and his duties would have included supervising the Tollbooth. The distance from her prison was only a few yards, but the bridge was thronged with people going to church since it was the Feast of the Annunciation, a Holy Day. The party who had been chosen to attend her death was Fawcett and Gibson, the two sheriffs, as well as a Protestant Minister and certain carefully screened witnesses. The actual execution was to be carried out by beggars and vagabonds, who no doubt would have been paid a few pence.

On entering her place of execution Margaret knelt and prayed. Her captors still played cat and mouse with her. They asked her to pray with them. The martyr realised their trap and replied firmly:

> 'I will not pray with you, and you shall not pray with me:
> neither will I say Amen to your prayer, nor you mine.'

Margaret then uttered her last prayers on this earth. She prayed for the Holy Catholic Church, and for the Pope and the Cardinals, and then for all Christian monarchs. Here she was interrupted and told to pray for the Queen. She then added:

'And especially for Elizabeth Queen of England, that God turn her the Catholic Faith, and after this mortal life she may receive the blessed joys of heaven.'

As the fatal act became close the junior sheriff, Gibson, was consumed with grief. He collapsed in tears and could not face his awful duty. His colleague, Fawcett, was made of sterner stuff and taunted Margaret even in her last moments. He said:

'Mrs. Clitherow, you must remember and confess you die for treason.'

The Saint retorted:

'No, no, Master sheriff, I die for the love of my Lord Jesu.'

Fawcett then demanded that she strip naked according to the judgement. Margaret and the women present begged him on their knees not to humiliate her by dying naked. One can speculate that Fawcett may have demanded this final degradation for a vicarious sexual thrill. Margaret was by all accounts a very beautiful woman. Fawcett refused their request. So the women unrobed the martyr and she lay down on the ground and a stout door was placed on top of her. Her hands were tied to two posts so that her body formed a perfect cross.

Even just before death her captors did not give up. They asked her to ask her husband's pardon, and by so doing inferred the foul slander that she had been unfaithful to him with the Catholic priests.

She said:

'If I have ever offended him, but for my conscience, I ask his forgiveness.'

Then the vagabonds did their work and placed great weights on the door. As the first weights went into position she uttered her last recorded words:

'Jesu, Jesu, Jesu, Have Mercy on Me!'

The Saint took about 15 minutes to die and had at least seven to eight hundredweights placed on her. Finally, her rib cage fractured and Margaret went to her God.

In this manner Saint Margaret Clitherow passed into the pages of history, and became an inspiration to all whom are oppressed for their belief.

> 'Can affliction or hardship? Can persecution, hunger, nakedness, peril, or the sword? "We are done to death for thy sake all day long", as Scripture says. "We have been treated like sheep for slaughter", and yet, in spite of all, overwhelming victory is ours through him who loved us. For I am convinced that there is nothing in death or life, in the realm of spirits or superhuman powers, in the world as it is or the world as it shall be, in the forces of the universe, in heights or depths, nothing in all creation that can separate us from the love of God in Christ Jesus our Lord.'
>
> *Romans 8 verses 35-39.*

Where lies her body?

Margaret's body was left under the press that killed her for about six hours. After this it was buried in secret, on a rubbish heap, within the confines of York. This was done to avoid Catholics having knowledge of where it was located, and hence being able to venerate her body.

The following reports give chapter and verse to these events:

'The persecutors having buried the Holy body under heaps of rubbish, endeavoured to keep the hiding place from all who might venerate it. The secret, however, was betrayed and a party of brave Catholic men, under the guidance, it is said of Father Mush, taking advantage of a dark and stormy night, six weeks after the martyrdom, with great labour, disinterred the precious remains and found them free of any taint of corruption. They were then carried by a man on horseback through the night a "great journey" and reburied in a place of which there is no record, probably in a mansion of one of the Old Catholic families of Yorkshire. It is hoped that the secret tomb may one day be discovered.'

Two further accounts are attributed to Grene's *Collectanea*:

'The body of Mrs. Clitherow being by her tormentors buried in a filthy place, the same night she was martyred, six weeks after a Catholic by diligent search found it and taking it up found it whole and without putrefaction. So carried it a great journey where he buried it again, more decently, eight weeks after her martyrdom, leaving her body so pure and uncorrupted, as though the blessed soul had departed from the body the day before, albeit it was so pressed and bruised as in order of her death set down.'

'Mrs. Clitherow's body was buried beside a dunghill in the town (York) where it lay full six weeks without putrefaction, by which times it was taken secretly by Catholics and carried on horseback, a long journey, to a place where it rested six days unbowelled, before necessary preservatives could be gotten. All of which time it remained without corruption or evil savour.'

It will be seen that there is strong degree of overlap between each of these three separate reports. This is not always the case with historic accounts of an event. The emphasis on the uncorrupted nature of Margaret's body is very important. This has been taken as a sign of sanctity since very early Christian times. Perhaps the best known case of an uncorrupted body was St. Cuthbert, bishop of Lindisfarne, who died in 687. It is claimed that his corpse remained pure and free of corruption for many centuries after his death, and that it looked like a man who had fallen asleep instead of one long dead.

Two traditions have built up over the years as to where Margaret lies buried. Perhaps the most well known claim is that she was buried at Hazlewood Castle. It is believed by many that, before her body was moved, her hand was cut off and this is preserved in the chapel of the Bar Convent to this day. Hazlewood Castle was the seat of the Vavasour family from the Middle Ages. It will be remembered that one of Margaret's closest friends was Dorothy Vavasour. Hazlewood is currently a luxurious hotel, with an international reputation and is roughly 13/14 miles from York. Some claim that this distance can not be called a 'great journey'. However, this judges the distance from York by modern standards. In 1586 the journey would have been over very crude tracks and could easily have taken a considerable time.

The other claim is that Margaret was interred at the Catholic chapel of Mount Grace at Osmotherly. This theory was given a considerable boost when in March, 1954, a skeleton was exhumed, which some believe may have been her body. It should be made quite plain that the author has no desire to enter into this controversy. It appears to be much more productive to allow readers to form their conclusions based on the evidence. The Osmotherly skeleton was found next to another body which was probably displaced, quite roughly, during its burial. The remains were found at a very shallow depth, only twenty-nine inches. There is some evidence to suppose that the grave was dug after the desecration of the chapel, since it has scraps of stained glass from the chapel's original windows. Furthermore, it would appear that the burial was at night, and thus in secret, since the remains of a candleholder have been found. The shallowness of the grave also indicates a rapid burial. The body was still wrapped in a fine linen shroud, with its arms extended along the flanks outside the thighs. It was tied in several directions with a silver cord. It has been established that this type of cord came from Elizabethan times and would have been available in 1586. The weave of the shroud shows it to be of Tudor origin. Either above or around the corpse was another wrapping that has been examined and which appears to be a quilt of birch bark. This has been used as a preservative for many centuries, certainly well before the Tudor period.

The body was in a light oak coffin. Coffins were rarely used in Elizabethan times unless a body was to be transported any distance. There are the remains of a chock found in the coffin to which the silver thread was attached and this it is believed could have secured the corpse when it was moved. Forensic examination in the 1950s showed that the skeleton belonged to a woman, that some of the ribs show evidence of fracture, and this might tie in with the nature of Margaret's death. However, opponents argue that they could have been fractured during burial, especially if this was in secret and at night.

Those who believe that this is the Saint's remains say that Margaret's body was wrapped in a bale of wool and carried on horseback down the old pack route from York to Newcastle. This passed very close to the chapel. However, a prominent authority at the time, Professor A. J. E. Cave, said that 'the age of death can not be less than forty years and is more probably 45-50 years'. It will be remembered that Margaret was probably around thirty-three at the time of her death. This view was based on the state of the bones, the evidence of quite advanced osteo-arthritis and food pockets in the jawbones as well as other technical points. It must be added that if the skeleton was examined today it might be possible to come up with more definite conclusions in view of the tremendous advances since the 1950s. It would, for instance, be possible to produce a replica of the face of the person based on the skull.

It was pointed out when the examination took place that Margaret could have contracted arthritis during her frequent prison sentences. Perhaps one of the most puzzling features was that the skeleton was of a person of 5ft 8 inches. Earlier in this book it was pointed out that most people in Elizabethan times were much smaller than today. If Margaret had been exceptionally tall it is very likely that this would have been mentioned in accounts of the time. Certainly there is a strong belief that she was petite, and many of her statues reflect this.

The Osmotherly skeleton has both hands. Reference has been made to the Bar Convent hand, which has a very strong oral and documented tradition. There is an old seventeenth-century document in the records of the Bar Convent that attests the validity of the hand as a relic of the Saint:

> 'Margaret Middleton (or her name in marryage Margaret Clitherow) was pressed to death by eight hundred pound weight for ye faith of Christ, which she bore with great constancy on ye 25 March 1586. Her body after death being thrown in a place of contempt. She was ye first of her sex who suffered martyrdom in the reign of Queen Elizabeth in England.'

Whatever, the true location of her body may be will probably never be known with certainty. It is perhaps easier to remember this brave, vibrant, and attractive woman from the many statues that exist of her. These may give us a greater feel for the Saint than any of her mortal remains.

Margaret in the Twentieth Century

The twentieth century was in many ways a period of vindication of Saint Margaret. It is certainly a period in which she was recognised by all religious traditions as a symbol of hope and ecumenism.

Without doubt the fulfilment of her martyrdom came on 25 October, 1970, when she was canonised by Pope Paul VI as one of the forty martyrs of England and Wales. This day is celebrated as their feast day.

Only twelve years on, in 1982, Pope John Paul II visited York on his tour of the United Kingdom. His visit was on 31 May, 1982. There was a huge open air Mass held on the Knavesmire, the sight of much martyrdom. In his homily the Pope covered the importance of family life in a secular society. He mentioned St. Margaret Clitherow, 'who gave her life in the City of York'. He cited her as a person whose 'call from God came in and through marriage and family life'.

The four-hundredth anniversary of her death brought Catholics and Anglicans together in a joint gesture of reconciliation and healing. There could probably be no greater tribute paid to her than this. On Easter Monday (24 March, 1986) a procession left the Anglican church of All Saints Pavement, a church Margaret would have known well. It made its way by way of the Shambles past the shrine that is believed to be her house, to York Minster. As the procession passed her home Anglicans and Catholics openly wept.

The procession was in many ways symbolic. At its head was the Lord Mayor of York, who was, of course, following in the line of her stepfather, Henry May. The Archbishop of York, Dr. John Habgood, and the Archbishop of Westminster, Cardinal Basil Hume, followed him. Also in the procession was Dr. Derek Warlock, the Archbishop of Liverpool. After this a service was held in York Minster, which was attended by thirteen Catholic bishops of England. This service marked a watershed in relations between Anglicans and Catholics.

Both Archbishop Habgood and Cardinal Hume placed much emphasis on reconciliation between the two Churches. In his sermon Dr. Habgood spoke movingly of Margaret's great courage and made the point that Christians still persecuted one another. In an oblique reference to Northern Ireland he added that the emotions that had been responsible for the death of a beautiful young woman were the same as those which applied in the twentieth century.

On Tuesday, 25 March, 1986, there was a commemoration Mass at St. Wilfrid's Church in the City centre to celebrate the life and martyrdom of St. Margaret Clitherow. On the same day, at Queen's Staith, the nearest location to the Tollbooth, an ecumenical service was held. Father Hugh Curristan, parish priest of English Martyrs

Church in York, took this. Father Curristan said very movingly in his homily: 'She was an example of what a true Christian should be. In her time and ours there was a yearning for true Christian values to be seen in someone with whom ordinary people could identify.' A Mass at Ampleforth Abbey was celebrated by Cardinal Basil Hume. At the same time there was an exhibition on the life of Margaret in the Guildhall in York, the place where she was sentenced to death.

Margaret has also, however, had a much more secular influence. In the 1950s in Boston, Massachusetts, USA, a play based on her life was performed *Design for a Stained Glass Window,* staged at the Wilbur Theatre in Boston. Martha Scott played the role of Margaret, while a young, then largely unknown, actor played her husband, John. His name was Charlton Heston. In a televised biography of Charlton Heston it was claimed he got the taste for historic drama from this play. Since he went on to play Moses, El Cid, Ben Hur, and St. Thomas More, Margaret may have influenced the film industry of this century. The play featured many people from Margaret's life, including Henry May, Father Mush, whose name was changed to Marsh! Also included were Anne Tesh and Judge Clinch. To appeal to animal lovers a dog called Azore was introduced, although its historical accuracy is very questionable.

Another play based on Margaret's life, *The White Rose,* has been produced. This was written by Dorothy O'Shea and was staged at Acocks Green in Birmingham. It also played in York.

It is wondered when some enterprising film director will take up the challenge of a film on the life and death of Margaret. Surely, it would have drama, deep emotion and the unusual attribute that it happens to be the truth.